D1445282

GROWING UP
with God's Friends

THE MUFFIN FAMILY

**GROWING UP
WITH GOD
SERIES ®**

V. GILBERT BEERS
Illustrated by HELEN ENDRES

HARVEST HOUSE PUBLISHERS
Eugene, Oregon 97402

GROWING UP WITH GOD'S FRIENDS

Copyright © 1987 by V. Gilbert Beers
Published by Harvest House Publishers
Eugene, Oregon 97402

Library of Congress Catalog Card
  Number 87-081046
ISBN 0-89081-528-3

Printed in the United States of America.

BEFORE YOU READ

GROWING UP WITH GOD'S FRIENDS is a book of Bible stories and Muffin Family stories about God's special friends, in Bible times and now. The Muffin Family, a family much like the one you want your family to be, shows how to live as God's friends should. Like the rest of us, they are not perfect, but they solve their problems the way God's friends should.

This book is part of the Muffin Family series, GROWING UP WITH GOD. Each story is really two stories—a Bible story, with a Bible truth about the way a Bible-time person lived for God, and a Muffin Family story with that same Bible truth at work in a family much like yours.

Each story emphasizes one important Bible teaching. At the heart of that Bible teaching is a moral and spiritual value—*forgiveness, patience, kindness, love, thankfulness,* and others.

At the end of each Bible story/Muffin story couplet, you will find two pages of Muffin application, to help you and your child apply the Bible teaching and moral/spiritual value to the life of your child.

A color-coding system helps you find your way through this book. The book has three sections, "God's Friends Are Good Friends," "God's Friends Are Good Neighbors," and "God's Friends Are Good Helpers." Each section has a different identifying color which begins on the contents page (What You Will Find in This Book) and continues throughout that section. Bible stories are identified with a color-coded line around the margin. Muffin Family stories have a color-coded bar at the bottom. And Muffin application pages have a color-coded line around the pages. Each section title page has a large color-coded border. Labels at the bottom of the pages identify A Muffin Bible Story, A Muffin Family Story, and A Muffin Application.

The Muffin Family Growing Up With God series consists of:

Growing Up With Jesus
Growing Up With My Family
Growing Up to Praise God
Growing Up With God's Friends

TO PARENTS AND TEACHERS

The Bible is an old book, written about people long ago and far away, people such as King David, Moses, Aaron, and Dorcas. But the Bible is also a book for today, and tomorrow. It is a book for you, and for your children. The Muffin Family books provide a bridge, or transition, between the people of the Bible and the children in your home and neighborhood.

Bible stories are retold in the language of today. Bible people come alive and your child will begin to feel at home in Dorcas' home or Abraham's tent. Your child will laugh with these people of long ago, play with them, and feel a part of their families.

Bible truth comes to life for today. What Moses learned from God is just as important for Mini Muffin and for your child.

From time to time you will see a make-believe story, a touch of fantasy. We clearly mark these places so your child will never confuse what is fact and what is fantasy. But fantasy is part of the fun of growing up.

So come with The Muffin Family into exciting adventures which will change your child's life. You'll be glad you did.

What You
Will Find
in This Book

GOD'S FRIENDS
ARE GOOD FRIENDS

- Jesus Needs Friends, Too! Matthew 26:30-56; Luke 22:39-53   8
  Where Are My Friends? *A Muffin Family Story*   11
  Muffin Application   14

- Gifts for a New Friend, 1 Samuel 17:55—18:4   16
  A Friend Far Away, *A Muffin Family Story*   18
  Muffin Application   20

- Onesimus—A New Friend, The Book of Philemon   22
  Friend or Servant? *A Muffin Family Story*   25
  Muffin Application   28

GOD'S FRIENDS
ARE GOOD NEIGHBORS

- A Different Kind of Neighbor, Acts 2:41-47   32
  Mini Happy Returns, *A Muffin Family Story*   35
  Muffin Application   38

- When King David Was a Bad Neighbor, 2 Samuel 11:1—12:14   40
  The Royal Feast, *A Muffin Make-believe Story*   43
  Muffin Application   46

- A Good Neighbor with Busy Hands, Acts 9:36-41   48
  Welcome Wagon, *A Muffin Family Story*   51
  Muffin Application   54

GOD'S FRIENDS
ARE GOOD HELPERS

- Timothy—A Good Helper, Acts 16:1-4; 1 & 2 Timothy   58
  A Toot and a Boom for the Prince, *A Muffin Make-believe Story*   61
  Muffin Application   64

- Helping Friends Far Away, Acts 2:38-47; 5:42; 8:5,6;
      26-39; 10:1-48; 13:1-6   66
  Sailing for Jesus, *A Muffin Family Story*   69
  Muffin Application   72

- Mary—God's Good Helper, Luke 1:26-38   75
  Mrs. Friggles' Helper, *A Muffin Family Story*   77
  Muffin Application   80

- A Surprise Helper, Luke 10:25-37   82
  The Almost Wasn't Helper, *A Muffin Family Story*   85
  Muffin Application   88

- Brothers Are Helpers, Exodus 4:18-31   90
  Two Hundred Bricks and Four Helpers,
      A Muffin Family Story   92
  Muffin Application   94

GOD'S FRIENDS
ARE GOOD FRIENDS

Jesus Needs Friends, Too!

Matthew 26:30-56;
Luke 22:39-53

"You will all run away from Me tonight," Jesus told His friends.

Jesus' friends stared at Him. Run away from Him? They couldn't do that! He was their best friend.

"I'll never run away from you," Peter said to Jesus.

"Before the rooster crows tomorrow morning, you will tell people three times that you do not even know Me," Jesus answered.

"Never!" Peter argued.

"Never!" the other friends said. But Jesus knew what would happen.

Jesus and His friends were in a quiet little garden on the Mount of Olives. It was called Gethsemane. They often came here to be alone, sometimes to pray together.

Tonight would be the last night they would be together before Jesus was crucified. Jesus' friends did not know this. But Jesus

did. That's why He had come here to pray with His friends.

Jesus took Peter, James, and John to another part of Gethsemane. "Stay here with Me while I pray," He told them. Then Jesus went a little farther to pray.

But when Jesus came back, the three friends were asleep. "Couldn't you stay awake one hour to pray with Me?" He asked. The three friends were ashamed. How could good friends do that?

Jesus prayed three times. But each time His friends did not pray with Him. They fell asleep instead.

Suddenly Jesus saw flickering torches coming across the valley from Jerusalem. He knew that His enemies were coming to get Him.

"Get up!" Jesus told His friends. "We are about to be betrayed."

A rough crowd came into the garden. There at the front of the crowd was Judas, one of Jesus' closest friends. Now Judas wasn't helping Jesus. He was helping Jesus' enemies.

"Who do you want?" Jesus asked.

"Jesus!" the crowd said.

"Here I am. Let My friends go," Jesus told the crowd. But He didn't need to say that. Already His friends were running away, just as He said they would.

When things go wrong, we need friends, don't we? Jesus needed friends, too! But they had all run away. Even Peter was gone now. Jesus did not have even one friend with Him as the crowd led Him back to Jerusalem.

Where Are
My Friends?

Maxi Muffin was so lonely. Where were his friends? They certainly weren't there with him. Maxi was sure that the old stump where he sat was his only friend.

The stars were beginning to appear in the evening sky. Maxi thought they looked friendly, but they were so far away. The warm yellow light from the windows of his house was friendly, too. But you can't play with warm yellow light.

Maxi began to think about his sad day. At breakfast he asked Mommi and Poppi to play a game. But Mommi had to go to the store and Poppi had chores to do.

When days start bad they keep on going that way. At least that's what Maxi decided.

At school recess time Maxi wanted to play with his friends Pookie, BoBo, and Tony, but they whispered and went away without him. The same thing happened at lunchtime. By afternoon recess, Maxi didn't even ask them to play with him.

When Maxi came home from school, Mini made a weak excuse and said she couldn't play. Mommi was busy cleaning the house, and Poppi wasn't home from work yet.

"So who else is there?" Maxi grumbled. "Ruff and Tuff are both sleeping, so I can't even play with my dog and cat!"

Maxi went out to the old stump to think and feel sorry for himself. He would be glad for even a mouse or chipmunk to squeak at him.

Suddenly Maxi heard a rustling behind him. "Ruff!" he squealed with delight. "You ARE my friend, aren't you?"

Maxi was still hugging Ruff when he heard more rustling behind him.

"Dinnertime, Maxi," said Mini. "I'll race you to the house!"

"Surprise! Surprise!" a chorus of voices sang out as Maxi ran into the house.

There were Maxi's friends—Pookie, BoBo, Tony, and Maria. Mommi and Poppi were there, too.

"It's hard to plan a surprise party for someone who wants to play all the time," they laughed. Do you think Maxi knew now that he had good friends?

Growing Is . . .
Being a Friend

What the Bible Story Teaches
Even Jesus needed friends in time of trouble.

Thinking about the Bible Story
1. Who told Jesus' friends that they would run away from Him?
2. When did they do that?
3. Why did Jesus need friends most at that time?

What the Muffin Story Teaches
We need friends, even though they do not always seem friendly.

Thinking about the Muffin Story
1. Why did Maxi think his friends had all gone away from him?
2. What were they doing when he wanted to play?
3. How did Maxi find that he really did have friends?

What Will A Good Friend Do?

Which of these do you want
a good friend to do for you?

1. Remember you on special days.
2. Stick with you when others don't.
3. Say bad things about you.
4. Help you know God better.
5. Pray for you.

The Bible Says
We should be kind to a friend who is hurting
(from Job 6:14).

Prayer
Dear Jesus, thank You for being
my special friend. Teach me how
to be a good friend to You and
others. Amen.

Gifts for a New Friend

1 Samuel 17:55—18:4

King Saul was excited when he saw David fight Goliath the giant. No man in his army was as brave as David. Who else would fight a giant like that with only a sling?

"What do you know about that young man?" the king asked General Abner.

"Nothing," said Abner.

"Then find out all you can," King Saul ordered.

Saul had promised that the man who killed Goliath would marry his daughter. David had killed the giant, so that's why Saul wanted to know more about him.

Abner hurried away to find David. He brought the young man to see the king.

"Tell me about your family," said the king.

"My father is Jesse," David answered. "Our home is at Bethlehem."

David was from a poor family. His father was only a shepherd. A shepherd boy did not usually marry a princess.

"Not one of my soldiers is as brave as you," Saul told David. "You were the only one who would fight Goliath."

While King Saul talked with David, Prince Jonathan sat nearby, listening. Jonathan was also a brave young man. Once he had fought a large band of Philistines, with only his armor bearer to help.

When David left King Saul, Jonathan went with him. "I want to be your best friend," he told David. "I will be like your brother as long as I live."

Then Jonathan gave David his beautiful cloak, his belt, his bow and arrows, and even his sword. "These will show that I want to be your friend," he said.

David and Jonathan agreed that they would never hurt each other. As long as they lived, they would be good friends and help each other. That's what good friends should do, isn't it?

A Friend
Far Away

"Mommi, do you have a friend you've never seen?" Mini asked.

"I suppose, Mini. Like who?"

"Oh, like someone faraway. Perhaps someone across the ocean."

"Hmmmm. Let me think, Mini. I really don't believe I have a friend like that."

"Mommi, may I have a friend across the ocean?"

"I suppose, Mini. Who are you thinking of?"

"The girl in this picture. My Sunday school teacher says she doesn't have enough food to eat or clothes to wear."

"Hmmmm. She really does need a friend, doesn't she?"

"Yes, Mommi. Our Sunday school class is going to help her. Some of us are giving half of our allowance all summer for her."

"Are you, Mini?"

"If it's OK with you, Mommi."

"I think that would be wonderful, Mini. Are you sure you want to do it?"

"Yes, Mommi. I don't want to give up my money, but I want to help my new friend."

"Will you write to her?"

"Oh, yes, Mommi. I want to tell her about my other friend."

"Other friend? Which one, Mini?"

"You know. My friend Jesus. Perhaps she will ask Him to become her friend too."

"Then she will have two new friends, Mini. That is even better than one friend, isn't it?"

"That's what I thought, too, Mommi. Oh

thank you, thank you."

"For what, Mini?"

"For being my wonderful mommi and knowing how I feel."

Growing Is . . .
Helping Friends

What the Bible Story Teaches
A good friend keeps on being a friend, no matter what happens.

Thinking about the Bible Story
1. How long did Jonathan want to be David's friend?
2. What did Jonathan give David to show that he would be his friend?
3. What did Jonathan and David agree they would never do to each other?

What the Muffin Story Teaches
Good friends like to do special things for each other.

Thinking about the Muffin Story
1. What did Mini want to do for her new friend?
2. What do you like to do for your friends?
3. What do you want your friends to do for you?

What Will You Do
When a Friend Needs You?

When a new friend or old friend needs you, which of these would you like to do?

1. Listen to your friend.
2. Talk with your friend.
3. Play with your friend.
4. Pray with your friend.
5. Make fun of your friend.

The Bible Says

A true friend is always a friend (from Proverbs 17:17).

Prayer

Dear Jesus, thank You for being my friend at all times. Teach me how to keep on being a friend to You and others. Amen.

Onesimus—A New Friend

The Book of Philemon

Paul's friend Philemon owned a slave named Onesimus. Many Bible-time people owned slaves. They bought slaves like horses or cattle. Some people were mean to their slaves. Others were kind. But a slave was a slave, no matter how he was treated.

Nobody knows why, but Onesimus ran away from Philemon. He went far away to Rome. There he met Paul, who was in prison. Paul told Onesimus how Jesus could forgive his sins and become his Savior.

Onesimus listened carefully. He wanted Jesus to forgive his sins. He wanted a Savior and Friend. So he accepted Jesus and became a Christian.

Now Onesimus began to help Paul. He

came often to the prison where Paul was kept. He ran errands for Paul. He was a good helper, always willing to do something for his new friend.

Onesimus also listened carefully as Paul taught him from God's Word. They often talked about Jesus and prayed together. They read God's Word and talked together about Jesus. Paul and Onesimus became good friends.

One day Onesimus looked sad when he came to see Paul. "I must tell you something," he confessed. "I am a runaway slave. Will you still be my friend?"

"Of course!" Paul said, smiling. "Haven't you been my friend, even though I am in prison? But who is your master?"

"Philemon," Onesimus answered.

"Philemon?" Paul was startled. "He's my friend. I helped him learn God's Word, just as I did for you. And I helped him accept Jesus as his Savior too."

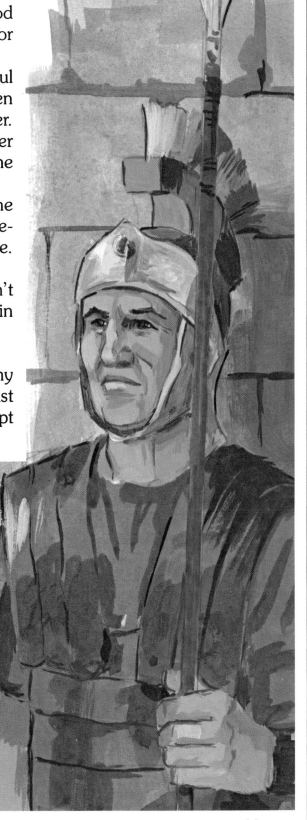

Now Onesimus felt even more sad. "What should I do?" he asked. "Should I go back and be his slave again?"

Paul thought for a long time. "And what should I do?" he wondered. "I have TWO good friends—a slave and his master. What SHOULD I do?"

Then Paul knew what he must do. He would write a letter to his friend Philemon. Onesimus would take it to him. That letter is in your Bible. It is called "Philemon."

"I thank God whenever I remember you," Paul wrote. Then Paul told how Onesimus had become his friend and had helped him.

"Please let him come back, not as a slave but as a friend," Paul asked Philemon.

Philemon loved Paul as a friend. So he must have welcomed Onesimus home as a friend too. That's what happens when Jesus is our friend, isn't it?

Friend or Servant?

A Muffin Make-believe Story about Muffkins of Muffkinland

In the land of the Muffkins there was a neighborhood like the one Maxi and Mini lived in. And there was a Maxi and Mini Muffkin, and Muffkins with the same names as their friends, such as BoBo and Tony.

One day BoBo Muffkin began to grumble and complain. "Why does Tony Muffkin

treat me like a servant?" he asked.

It was true. Whenever Tony Muffkin said "do this," BoBo Muffkin did it. Whenever Tony Muffkin said "do that," BoBo Muffkin did that too.

"But why?" he often asked.

One day BoBo stopped grumbling. That's because he stopped doing things for Tony. Instead, he went for a long walk.

"Why?" he kept asking as he walked.

"Why what?" a voice answered. Then BoBo saw his friend Maxi Muffkin.

"Why does Tony Muffkin treat me like a servant instead of a friend?" said BoBo.

"How do you treat Tony Muffkin, like a friend or a master?" asked Maxi Muffkin.

"I . . . I . . ." BoBo Muffkin tried to answer. Suddenly he knew what was wrong. He was treating Tony Muffkin like a master. That's why Tony was treating him like a servant.

"Let's go see Tony," said Maxi Muffkin.

They found Tony Muffkin, still munching on a hamburger BoBo Muffkin had brought him. "Hey kid," Tony Muffkin said to BoBo Muffkin, "get me some lemonade, will you?"

Maxi Muffkin looked angry. "Why didn't you say that to me?" he asked.

"Because you're my friend," said Tony Muffkin. "I wouldn't say that to a friend."

Suddenly Tony knew what he had said. He looked at BoBo. He wanted to be his friend, not his master.

"I'm sorry, my FRIEND," Tony Muffkin said to BoBo Muffkin.

"That's all right, my FRIEND," BoBo answered.

Then Tony Muffkin went to get BoBo Muffkin a glass of lemonade so he could sit by the pool.

Aren't you glad that BoBo Muffkin wrote all this down so you could read it? And aren't you glad that Tony Muffkin always treated BoBo Muffkin like a friend from that time until this. That's the way it should be, isn't it?

Growing Is . . .
Being Kind to Friends

What the Bible Story Teaches

If you want someone to be your friend, you must be kind to that person.

Thinking about the Bible Story

1. Who were Paul's two friends?
2. How did they know each other?
3. What did Onesimus do for Paul?
4. What did Paul ask Philemon to do for him and Onesimus?

What the Muffin Story Teaches

If you are going to call someone a friend, you should treat that person like a friend, not like a servant.

Thinking about The Muffin Story

1. How did Tony Muffkin usually treat BoBo Muffkin, like a friend or like a servant?
2. What did Maxi say to BoBo?
3. What did Tony do then? Why?

What Should a Good Friend Not Do?

Which of these should you not do to a good friend?

1. Make fun of your friend.
2. Steal from your friend.
3. Say bad things to others about your friend.
4. Help your friend when he's in trouble.
5. Ask your friend to do something wrong.

The Bible Says

Be kind to each other, treating each other like brothers (from Romans 12:10).

Prayer

Dear Jesus, I really do want You to be my very best friend. Show me how to be a kind and loving friend to each person I call my friend. Amen.

GOD'S FRIENDS ARE GOOD NEIGHBORS

A Different Kind of Neighbor

Acts 2: 41-47

"They are so different from our other neighbors," some people in Jerusalem said.

These people were talking about Jesus' followers. It was true. They were different. But they were different in a wonderful way.

Most neighbors earned as much and kept as much as they could. Jesus' followers gave it away. Most neighbors helped themselves. Jesus' followers helped others. Most neighbors bragged about themselves and their families. Jesus' followers told others how Jesus had changed their lives.

Something else was different. Most neighbors were never very happy. They complained about this and grumbled about that. There was never enough of some things and always too much of other things. But Jesus' followers were the happiest people in town.

That's why the neighbors said Jesus' followers were different. That's why the neighbors wondered if they should become Jesus' followers also.

Jesus had told His followers that this would happen. "You will receive power when the Holy Spirit comes," He said. The Holy Spirit came and Jesus' followers received His power. That's what made them different.

Each day more people began to follow Jesus. They let the Holy Spirit go with them. Then their neighbors saw how different they were. And those neighbors wanted to follow Jesus too.

Soon there were many people who followed Jesus. Don't you think Jesus' followers were glad they had been good neighbors? Don't you think they were glad they had been a little different from the other neighbors?

Mini Happy Returns

"Happy birthday, Mrs. Grump!" Mini Muffin said to the pretend Mrs. Grump in her mirror, who was just Mini's reflection.

"Why, thank you dearie," Mrs. Grump smiled sweetly at Mrs. Grunt, who was really Mini Muffin pretending to be Mrs. Grunt.

"Since you're such a DEAR friend, I'm making a devil's food cake for your birthday," said Mrs. Grunt.

"DEVIL'S food? Of all the nerve! Is that what you think of me, dearie? And why not ANGEL food?"

"Hrummph! Angel! But were you an angel last week when you gossiped to the neighbors about me?"

"So now I'm a gossip! I'm mortified! I was just telling my neighbors some important things about my DEAR friend!"

Each part of the conversation went up one notch higher and one notch louder. Ruff and Tuff came to see what was going on.

Suddenly Ruff snarled at Mrs. Grump. Tuff hissed at Mrs. Grunt.

Before long, Mrs. Grump and Mrs. Grunt became nasty. They began to say some very un-Muffinlike things to each other.

As things became louder and hotter, Tuff and Ruff became angry at each other. Suddenly Tuff jumped on Ruff and scratched his nose. Then Ruff got Tuff on the floor and began to teach her how an angry dog fights.

"Happy grouchday!" Mrs. Grunt shouted.

"You're as half-baked as your cakes, dearie," Mrs. Grump shouted back.

At the loudest part of the Grump-Grunt-Ruff-Tuff argument, Mommi walked in. Her mouth fell open and her eyes opened wide.

"WHATEVER is happening here?" Mommi almost had to shout above the noise.

Suddenly Mrs. Grump smiled sweetly at Mrs. Grunt and thanked her for the LOVEly devil's food cake. This caused Mrs. Grunt to smile just as sweetly. She told Mrs. Grump that her angel food cake would be simply DElicious.

Just as suddenly Ruff stopped fighting Tuff and Tuff stopped fighting Ruff. Ruff plopped down in his corner, looked at Tuff with one cautious eye, yawned, and went to sleep. Tuff plopped into her basket, glanced once more at Ruff, yawned, and went to sleep.

"NOW, Mini Muffin, please tell me what was going on in here!"

"Oh, nothing much, Mommi. We were just having a little birthday party. But it did get out of hand, so we'll tell everyone to be sweet to each other from now on."

"Hmmmm. All right, then. Mini happy returns."

Growing Is . . .
Being a Friendly Neighbor

What the Bible Story Teaches
When Jesus is our friend, we will help our neighbors become Jesus' friends too.

Thinking about the Bible Story
1. How were Jesus' followers different from their neighbors?
2. How did Jesus' followers help their neighbors become Jesus' friends?
3. How were Jesus' followers good neighbors?

What the Muffin Story Teaches
If you want your neighbors to be friends, you must first be friendly.

Thinking about the Muffin Story
1. Were Mrs. Grump and Mrs. Grunt kind to each other?
2. Why did each get angry whenever the other was unkind?
3. What would have happened if either had stopped quarreling?

How Can I Be Friendly to My Neighbors?

How can you show your neighbors that you are friendly?

1. Smile at my neighbors.
2. Talk nice to my neighbors.
3. Do something good for my neighbors.
4. Yell at my neighbors.
5. Tell my neighbors I want to be their friend.

The Bible Says
Love your neighbor as you love yourself (from Leviticus 19:18).

Prayer
Dear Jesus, come with me while I am with my neighbors. I want them to know You are my friend. Amen.

When King David Was a Bad Neighbor

2 Samuel 11:1—12:14

Usually King David was a good man. He loved God and tried to please Him. He even wrote many wonderful psalms.

But even the best people sometimes do wrong things. One time King David did something very wrong to some neighbors.

It all started when David's army went out to fight. Uriah, one of the young army officers, went with the army. His beautiful wife Bathsheba stayed home, which was near King David's palace.

David saw Bathsheba one evening and was sure that she was the most beautiful woman in the world. The more he thought about Bathsheba, the more he wanted to treat her like his wife. But of course she was already married to Uriah.

One day David could stand it no longer. He sent for Bathsheba and made her pretend that she was his wife, not Uriah's wife. The king was being a very bad neighbor. He was also sinning against God.

Sin makes things worse, not better. One day Bathsheba told David they were going to have a baby. Now the king knew what a mess he had made. Instead of saying "I'm sorry," he brought Uriah home and tried to get him to stay with his wife. He wanted Uriah to think this was his baby.

But Uriah would not go to his home while his friends were fighting. David's plan failed.

Now King David covered up one sin with a bigger one. He ordered Uriah's commanding officer to send him into a place where he would be killed.

When Uriah was dead, King David was free to marry Bathsheba. But that was not the end of David's troubles. The prophet Nathan came to see him one day. He told David a story about a rich man who had a feast. Instead of cooking his own lamb, he killed a poor man's pet lamb and ate it.

David was very angry. "That man will be punished!" he shouted.

"You're right," said Nathan. "You are that man." Then Nathan reminded David that he had killed Uriah so he could have his wife.

"I have sinned!" King David cried out. "I have sinned against God."

It was true. David's sin had hurt Uriah. It had hurt Bathsheba. It had hurt him. It would hurt the baby they would have, because Nathan said it would die. But most of all, David's sin hurt God, as all sin does.

David had been a bad neighbor. He could never repay Uriah for the hurt he had caused. He could never bring back the baby. But David did ask God to forgive him. And he would always be a better neighbor to those around him.

The Royal Feast

A Muffin Make-believe Story about a Royal Kingdom Far Away

"Saddle our horses, Sir Pookie," King Maxi ordered. "We will search for a lamb for the royal feast."

"But you don't need horses to look at your lambs," said Sir Pookie. "They're here at the royal palace."

"Who knows where we will find the lamb we need?" said King Maxi.

Sir Pookie did not like to hear that. But he did not want to ask more questions. Knights were important, but kings were more important. Sometimes knights who asked kings too many questions were not knights very long.

Before long, King Maxi and Sir Pookie rode across the drawbridge and out into the country.

They passed the rich house of Sir Anthony of Squireshire, whom the king called Tony. They went by the estate of Sir Charles of Willow Manor. The king called him Charlie.

"Have you seen the lamb yet?" Sir Pookie asked.

"Not yet," said King Maxi. "But I will know it when I see it."

They were far into the country now, where poor people lived in little huts. "How do you expect to find the best lamb out here?" Sir Pookie asked.

"Who knows?" said the king. "It could be anywhere. It could even be that lamb playing with that little girl over there."

King Maxi stopped and watched the lamb. The girl was having so much fun with it. "You are my dear pet," she said. "I love you like my best friend."

"That's the lamb," said the king. "Get it for me."

"But it is a pet lamb," Sir Pookie argued.

The girl cried out as they took her lamb away. "No, no! You must not take my pet lamb," she cried.

When they reached the castle, King Maxi called for the royal executioner to kill the lamb. He called for the royal chef to cook it for the feast. But before the executioner came, Princess Mini walked up.

"Guess what happened while you were gone?" she said. "A wicked boy stole our Tuff and plans to make catburgers with her."

King Maxi was furious. "I'll boil him in oil," he shouted. "I'll . . . I'll . . ."

"Before you blow a royal fuse, tell me why you're so angry," Princess Mini asked.

"Because Tuff was our pet," said the king. "Now tell me who did this terrible thing."

"You!" said Princess Mini. "But it wasn't Tuff, it was that poor girl's lamb. Now give it back before I fry you for the royal feast."

Before long the girl had the lamb safe in her arms. Then King Maxi invited her to stay for the royal feast—hamburgers, fries, and shakes.

Growing Is . . .
Being a Good Neighbor

What the Bible Story Teaches
When we are not good neighbors we can hurt them and ourselves. We can hurt God too.

Thinking about the Bible Story
1. What did David do that hurt his neighbors?
2. How did this hurt Uriah? How did it hurt Bathsheba?
3. How did this hurt David? How did it hurt God?

What the Muffin Story Teaches
It is wrong to do something that hurts our neighbors or friends.

Thinking about the Muffin Story
1. How does the Muffin story remind you of David and Bathsheba?
2. How was King Maxi like King David?
3. How was Princess Mini like Nathan?
4. How did King Maxi make things right?

Are You a Good Neighbor?

If you did something to hurt your neighbor, which of these would you do?

1. Tell your neighbor you're sorry.
2. Ask your neighbor to forgive you.
3. Help your neighbor do something good.
4. Tell your neighbor it's his fault.

The Bible Says

Do not plan to hurt your neighbor (from Proverbs 3:29).

Prayer

Dear Jesus, keep me from doing wrong things that would hurt my friends and neighbors. But if I do, please forgive me. Amen.

A Good Neighbor with Busy Hands

Acts 9:36-41

"Who has the busiest hands in Joppa?" people asked.

"Dorcas, of course," was the answer.

Her name wasn't really Dorcas. It was Tabitha. But her friends and neighbors called her Dorcas, which meant antelope. She was always running like an antelope to help others.

Dorcas never had time to do good things for herself. She was always too busy helping others. Everyone loved the woman with the busy hands. Why shouldn't they?

"When my little girl was sick, Dorcas was the first one there," a woman said.

"And did you see the lovely clothes she made for us?" said another.

When Dorcas wasn't nursing sick people or making clothes for poor people, she was taking food to someone who didn't have enough, or helping an older friend clean her house.

In all Joppa, there was no one like Dorcas. And in all Joppa no one was loved more than Dorcas.

But one day something sad happened. "Have you heard?" someone whispered.

"No, not Dorcas. What will we do without her?" said another.

With sad hearts some women prepared her body to be buried. "If Peter were here, he would know what to do," they whispered.

Then someone had an idea. "Peter isn't far away. He's visiting at Lydda now. Perhaps someone could find him."

Before long some men came back with

Peter. But what sad friends. It looked like all Joppa had come there to cry.

"Please, all of you leave the room," Peter said.

When they left, Peter knelt beside Dorcas' body. He talked with God about her and her friends. Then tenderly he spoke to Dorcas.

"Dorcas, you may get up now," he said.

Slowly Dorcas opened her eyes and saw Peter standing there beside her. But why was she lying there when she had guests?

"Oh, I'm sorry," she said. "I must have been sleeping. I will hurry and get something for you to eat."

Peter whispered, "Come with me first."

Peter took Dorcas by the hand and led her downstairs where her friends were waiting. They could hardly believe their eyes. There was Dorcas, alive and well. God had brought her back to life again.

There was never so much excitement in Joppa. Never! Wherever people went, they talked about the wonderful thing that had happened to Dorcas. Dorcas thought it was wonderful too. Now she could keep on helping her friends and neighbors.

Welcome Wagon

"Mommi! Poppi!" Mini Muffin shouted. "Some people are moving into the empty house down the street. And guess what? Their other house burned, so they have almost nothing to move here."

"Oh," said Mommi. "How sad to lose all you have in a fire."

"We should do something to help them," said Poppi. "But what?"

"I know," said Mommi. "I'll call all the ladies in the neighborhood. We'll have a shower for them. It will certainly help to have a few new things for their house."

While Mommi talked about her shower, Maxi and Mini went into the yard. "What can we do, Maxi?" Mini asked.

"Well it can't be some old shower," said

Maxi. "That's for girls!"

Maxi and Mini sat in the yard for a long time, trying to think of some way to help the new neighbors. Suddenly Mini looked up at a car going by. There were words painted on the side.

"What's a Welcome Wagon?" Mini asked.

"Someone in there will go to see the new neighbors," said Maxi. "They will take some things to help them know more about the town."

"That's it!" said Mini. "We'll fix up a Welcome Wagon for the children."

It was such a good idea that Maxi couldn't think of a thing wrong with it. So he and Mini got their little red wagon from the garage. They put an orange crate on the wagon and hung a sign on it that said "Welcome Wagon."

"This will be fun," said Mini. As soon as they told Mommi and Poppi about their idea, they started down the street.

"Give a toy to the Welcome Wagon," they said to each of their friends. So each friend gave a good toy to take to the new neighbor children. Before long the orange crate on the Welcome Wagon was filled with toys.

When the new neighbor children opened their door, they could hardly believe their eyes. "Surprise!" said Mini and Maxi.

"Just like Dorcas," said the new mother when she saw Maxi and Mini.

"Do you know about Dorcas?" they asked.

"Yes, we're Jesus' friends too," she said.

Don't you think Dorcas would have been pleased with Maxi and Mini?

Growing Is . . .
Helping Neighbors

What the Bible Story Teaches

God's friends like to help their neighbors by doing good things for them.

Thinking about the Bible Story

1. What kind of person was Dorcas? Why do you think people loved her?
2. Why do you think Dorcas did good things for her neighbors?
3. What did Dorcas' busy hands say about her love for God?

What the Muffin Story Teaches

When neighbors need us, God wants us to help them.

Thinking about the Muffin Story

1. How were Maxi and Mini like Dorcas?
2. What did Mini and Maxi do to help their new neighbors?
3. Why do you think the new neighbors were glad for Maxi's and Mini's help?

How Can You Help Your Neighbors?

What should you do to help a neighbor?

1. Vacuum or dust for an older person.
2. Go to the store for a neighbor who can't get out.
3. Throw stuff on your neighbor's lawn.
4. Help a neighbor do something special that he or she can't usually do.
5. Go with a neighbor to a special place.

The Bible Says

Whoever helps needy people honors God (from Proverbs 14:31).

Prayer

Dear Jesus, show me some needy person I can help, then be with me as I try to help that person. Amen.

GOD'S FRIENDS ARE
GOOD HELPERS

Timothy—A
Good Helper

**Acts 16:1-4;
1 & 2 Timothy**

"Who is that handsome young man?"
Paul asked some friends.

"Timothy," they answered.

"The name sounds Greek," said Paul.

"His father is Greek, but his mother is
Jewish," they said. "You should meet that
woman. Eunice has read the Bible and prayed
with Timothy since he was a baby. So has
Timothy's grandmother Lois."

Before long Paul met these two wonderful

women. While he was staying there at Lystra, he met many of their friends too. He told these people that Jesus was God's Son and that He wanted to be their Savior.

Eunice and Lois accepted Jesus as their Savior. So did Timothy. And so did many others at Lystra.

The next time Paul came to Lystra his friends told how Timothy had been doing many good things for Jesus there.

"I need someone like Timothy to go with me and help me do Jesus' work," said Paul. "What a good helper he would be."

Timothy was glad to become Paul's helper. But Paul told him it would not be easy. "Some people do not like what I say about Jesus," he warned. "Some want to hurt me or even kill me. Do you still want to go?"

"Of course," said Timothy. He wanted to be Paul's helper and work for Jesus. He wanted to do this even if he got hurt.

Timothy went many places with Paul. He helped Paul work for Jesus in many ways.

"What a helper," Paul often said.

Sometimes Paul sent Timothy to a faraway city. Sometimes he told Timothy to stay while he went far away.

Once Timothy got a letter from Paul. He told Timothy he had been put into prison in Rome.

"I pray for you every day," Paul told Timothy. "I want to see you very much. I know how you trust God as your mother, Eunice, and grandmother Lois do. Please come and bring my cloak and books."

Timothy must have hurried to Rome to see Paul. He must have taken what Paul needed.

"What a good helper you are," Paul told him. And he was!

A Toot and a Boom for the Prince

A Muffin Make-believe Story
about Muffkins of Muffkinland

Have you ever seen a parade? But what would a parade be without horns tooting and drums booming? It really would not be a good parade, would it?

Now you know why a Muffkin parade is so special. You have never heard such tooting and booming in all your life.

If you came to this Muffkin parade today you would see a Muffkin with a golden horn, tooting as only a Muffkin golden-horn tooter can toot. And you would see a Muffkin with a royal drum, booming as only a Muffkin royal-drum boomer can boom. And of course there is always a Muffkin clanging cymbals until you have to hold your ears.

Muffkins from all over Muffkinland came to hear all the wonderful tooting and booming. This went on until the tooters and boomers could hardly make one sound.

Just then a Muffkin ran from the palace. "Please, come with me," he said. "The prince is sick. He wants to hear your wonderful music. That will help him get well."

The Muffkin tooters and boomers were so tired. They really wanted to go home. But they also wanted to be good helpers. If they could help their Muffkin prince get well, they would do it.

So the Muffkin tooters and boomers picked up their instruments and hurried to the palace. There was the prince, waiting on his balcony for them.

As soon as the Muffkin musicians saw the prince, they began marching. They tooted and boomed better than they had done all day. They wanted to help their prince get well.

"Wonderful music!" the prince shouted. "Wonderful friends! Thank you for coming to help me get well."

Tooters and boomers really are good helpers, aren't they?

Growing Is . . .
Being Good Helpers

What the Bible Story Teaches
We like to help Jesus' friends because that is helping Jesus.

Thinking about the Bible Story
1. How did Timothy help Paul?
2. How did this help Jesus?
3. How did Timothy's mother and grandmother help him become a good helper?
4. Do you think Timothy helped Paul because he loved him? Do you think he helped Paul because he loved Jesus?

What the Muffin Story Teaches
Good helpers enjoy helping when they love the person they are helping.

Thinking about the Muffin Story
1. Why did the musicians want to play for the prince?
2. How were they like Timothy?

We Show Love by Being Good Helpers

In the picture below, the Muffin family is showing love to each other by being good helpers. But how?

1. Are the Muffins helping to wash dishes?
2. Are they helping to plant a flower?
3. Are they helping each other?
4. Are they helping Jesus?

The Bible Says

Help one another because you love one another (from Galatians 5:13).

Prayer

Dear Jesus, I love You, so I want to help You and Your friends. Show me how, then teach me do my best. Amen.

Helping Friends Far Away

**Acts 2:38-47;
5:42; 8:5-6,
26-39; 10:1-48; 13:1-6**

People everywhere were talking about Jesus. Thousands had become His followers and were telling their friends and neighbors about Him.

The excitement went far beyond Jerusalem. People in Samaria believed when Philip preached to them. An Ethiopian officer believed when Philip sat in his chariot, telling him about Jesus. Even Cornelius, a Roman officer in Caesarea, accepted Jesus into his life.

Far to the north, in the city of Antioch, some of Jesus' followers started a church. There were important people in this church, even a man named Manaen who had grown up with King Herod.

These Christians met often to pray. They wanted to know what they could do to please Jesus the most.

One day when these people were praying, the Holy Spirit spoke to them. They listened carefully, for they wanted more than anything to obey God.

"Send Barnabas and Paul out to work for Me," He told them.

So these people had a special church meeting. They placed their hands on Barnabas and Paul. "Go where He leads you,"

they said. "May God be with you."

Barnabas and Paul prayed for the Holy Spirit to go with them. They wanted to be God's helpers in the faraway places where God would send them. They wanted to help the people in faraway places know Jesus.

As the ship sailed away, taking Barnabas and Paul to other places, they must have wondered where God would lead them. And how could they know that thousands would accept Jesus because they were God's faithful helpers?

Sailing for Jesus

"Poppi."

"Yes, Mini."

"May Maxi and I sail to faraway lands like Paul did?"

"How will you get there, Mini?"

"Oh, Maxi will make a strong ship, like a raft. It will be big enough for both of us."

"To sail across the ocean?"

"Oh, yes, Poppi. We'll go to faraway places and tell people about Jesus. We'll tell them how Jesus loves them and how He wants them to love Him too."

"Do you think they will listen to you?"

"Of course, Poppi. Maxi will preach and I'll sing."

"Mini."

"Yes, Poppi."

"Not all the people listened to Paul. Some of them threw big rocks at him. They hated him because he told them about Jesus."

"That's OK. Maxi and I don't mind. We'll keep our ship ready so we can sail away to other places when people get mean."

"Mini."

"Yes, Poppi."

"Why do you want to do this?"

"My Sunday school teacher says many of these people don't love Jesus. Anyway, it will be fun to sail to faraway places, too."

"Mini."

"Yes, Poppi."

"Is it just as much fun to tell people about Jesus if they don't live far away?"

"I . . . I guess so, Poppi. Like where?"

"Oh, like down the street or across town."

"But Poppi, do they need Jesus as much as the people far away?"

"Yes, Mini. They need Him just as much. And the people far away need Him just as much as our neighbors too. They all need Him the same."

"Then why do people go far away to tell people about Jesus? Why don't they stay home and talk to their neighbors?"

"Mini, if everyone stayed home, how would the faraway people hear about Jesus? And if everyone went far away, how would the people at home hear about Jesus?"

"So we need some people to go far away and some people to talk with the neighbors?"

"Right, Mini."

"Poppi."

"Yes, Mini."

"Maybe Maxi and I can talk with our neigh-

bors now about Jesus. Then later we can sail far away to tell those people."

"I'm glad you want to tell people everywhere about Jesus, Mini. But now it's time to sleep."

"Goodnight, Poppi."

"Goodnight, Mini."

Growing Is . . .
Helping Others Far and Near

What the Bible Story Teaches

Jesus wants us to tell others far and near that He loves them.

Thinking about the Bible Story

1. Why did Barnabas and Paul go far away? Why didn't they just stay home?
2. Who asked them to go on this trip?
3. Who did they want to go with them? How did they ask Him?

What the Muffin Story Teaches

We want to tell others about Jesus because we love Him.

Thinking about the Muffin Story

1. Who needs to hear about Jesus?
2. Must we always go far away to tell people about Jesus? Why not?
3. What would happen if no one went far away to tell people about Jesus?

How Should We Tell People about Jesus?

Which of these should we do to help people know Jesus?

1. Tell people what God's Word says.
2. Show people how God's people should live.
3. Make them believe in Jesus.
4. Help people know that we love them.

The Bible Says

Say things that will help build others up (from Ephesians 4:29).

Prayer

Thank You, Jesus, for all You have done for me. I love You and want to tell others what You can do for them. Amen.

Mary—God's Good Helper

Luke 1:26-38

"Mary," a voice said softly.

Mary jumped up and looked around the room. She was surprised and afraid to hear a voice. She was alone in her room, praying to God.

"Who . . . who are you?" Mary whispered.

"I am the angel Gabriel," the voice answered. "I have good news for you."

Mary was frightened. She had never seen an angel before. Now she was talking with Gabriel, one of the chief angels of heaven.

"Don't be afraid," Gabriel said. "God has chosen you to help Him in a special way."

"Me?" Mary whispered. "What special work could I help God do?"

"God wants you to have a baby boy," said the angel. "This baby will be the Messiah, God's Son. He will be the Savior!"

Mary could hardly speak. Her people had

prayed for hundreds of years for the Messiah to come. Now Gabriel was telling her that she would be the Messiah's mother.

"But Joseph and I are not married yet," she said. "How can I have a baby?"

"This will not be Joseph's son," Gabriel said. "He will be God's Son."

Mary began to wonder. What would she say to Joseph? What would he do? Would he believe her? Who would believe her?

Suddenly these things did not matter. "I will do whatever God wants me to do," said Mary.

Then Mary must have prayed, "Thank You for letting me be Your special helper."

Mrs. Friggles' Helper

"I'm so glad you have no school this afternoon, Mini," said Mommi. "I have something you can do for me."

Mini looked as sour as a green apple when Mommi said that. "I have one afternoon off and I have to work," she thought. But she didn't say it to Mommi.

"What can I do for you?" Mini asked.

"I'm really sorry to ask you to do this today," said Mommi. "But I need your help. Mrs. Friggles can't get out of the house to shop. I've made a dozen plastic containers of stew for her. If you will take them over in your wagon, I will appreciate it."

Mini was still looking glum when she loaded her wagon with the plastic containers, which Mommi put into two grocery bags. "Did you have something special you wanted to do this afternoon?" Mommi asked.

"Well, I wanted to go to Maria's house," said Mini. "She just got a miniature tea set for her birthday. It's just like the one you had when you were a little girl."

"Is it an antique?" Mommi asked.

"No, that really would be special," said Mini. "It's just a new one from the department store downtown."

"I'm sorry," said Mommi. "I can't take the stew, Poppi is at work, and Maxi is at baseball practice. So you see, Mrs. Friggles needs you."

"I'll just have to wait to play with Maria's tea set," said Mini. "And Mommi, sometime I would love a tea set like that for Christmas or my birthday."

Mommi smiled. She thought of the tea set as Mini went down the sidewalk with her wagonload of stew. Mommi remembered the tea set she had when she was a little girl.

Mini was still feeling glum when she pulled her wagon up to Mrs. Friggles' door. "This seems halfway across town," Mini thought.

Mrs. Friggles was so glad to see Mini and the stew. "Your mother is so sweet to think of me," she said. "I can't walk much these days. So it's quite a help when someone does something special for me."

Mini carried the plastic containers into Mrs. Friggles' house and helped her put them in the refrigerator. She was almost ready to leave when she noticed how different Mrs. Friggles' house looked. Mommi always kept her house so clean and Mrs. Friggles' house looked so messy.

Mrs. Friggles saw Mini looking around. "It is a bit messy," she said. "I'm sorry. I'm not well enough to clean the house myself, and I can't afford to hire someone."

Mini was almost out of the door when she looked around again. Then she looked at Mrs. Friggles, sitting in her chair. Mini felt sorry for her. It must be awful to have to sit there and look at a messy house all day.

"Do you have a vacuum cleaner?" Mini asked.

"Yes . . . yes I do," said Mrs. Friggles. "I keep it in the closet over there."

"Well, first I'll call Mommi and tell her I'll be home a little later," Mini said. "Then I'll help you tidy things up a little."

Mrs. Friggles watched from her chair as Mini vacuumed the rug carefully from one

end to the other. Then Mini washed the dishes in the kitchen sink and cleaned all the furniture tops. Mini grunted and groaned a little as she sprayed each window with glass cleaner and rubbed it until it sparkled. Then at last she flopped down in a big chair next to Mrs. Friggles.

"Whew!" she said. "That's about all I can do in one day."

"Bless you, child," said Mrs. Friggles. "You did more work here this afternoon than I could do in the next two months."

Mini gave Mrs. Friggles a big hug and headed for the door. She was so glad she had been Mrs. Friggles' special helper.

"Wait," said Mrs. Friggles. "There's just one more little thing you can do for me." Mini was sure she was too tired to do one more thing, but ran back anyway.

"Open that top drawer over there and bring me the blue box," said Mrs. Friggles.

Mrs. Friggles smiled as she opened the box. Inside was a beautiful antique miniature tea set.

This was mine when I was a little girl," she said. "I always wanted a granddaughter to give it to. But I never had one. Today you have been a special granddaughter to me."

Mini's heart sang all the way home. She could hardly wait to show Mommi the really special gift from her new grandmother.

Growing Is . . .
Helping When It Hurts

What the Bible Story Teaches
God wants us to help Him, even when it may hurt us.

Thinking about the Bible Story
1. What special work did God ask Mary to do? Why?
2. How did God tell Mary about this special work?
3. Was Mary willing to do God's special work? Why?

What the Muffin Story Teaches
We should be God's helper even when we have to give up something we want.

Thinking about the Muffin Story
1. What did Mommi ask Mini to do? What did Mini have to give up to do this?
2. What extra work did Mini do that Mommi had not asked her to do? Why was that being a good helper?
3. Did Mini expect a reward for helping? What reward did she get?

What Did Maxi and Mini Give Up?

Mini and Maxi are helping Mommi and Poppi today. What do you think they have given up to help?

1. Playing with friends.
2. Getting ice cream at Pop's Sweet Shop.
3. Sleep, because it is night.
4. Eating dinner with Mommi and Poppi.

The Bible Says

Be glad that you can help God (from Psalm 100:2).

Prayer

Dear Jesus, let me help You because I love You. And let me help my family and friends because I love them too. Amen.

A Surprise Helper

Luke 10:25-37

"What must I do to live forever?" a man asked Jesus one day. It was a trick question. This man wanted Jesus to say the wrong thing about the religious law. The man knew much about the law and thought he could trap Jesus.

"You should know the answer to that," Jesus said. "What do you find in the law about that?"

"Love God with all your heart, soul, strength and mind," said the man. "And love your neighbor as yourself."

"You have given the right answer," Jesus told him. "If you do this, you will live forever."

But the man still wanted to trick Jesus, so he asked another question. "But who is my neighbor?" he asked.

Then Jesus told this story to answer the man's question:

"One of our own Jewish men was traveling on the road from Jerusalem to Jericho when robbers jumped on him. They took his clothes and money, beat him, and left him half-dead by the road.

"Not long after that, one of our own priests came along the road. When he saw this man, he passed by on the other side of the road. Then a Levite, who helps our religious work,

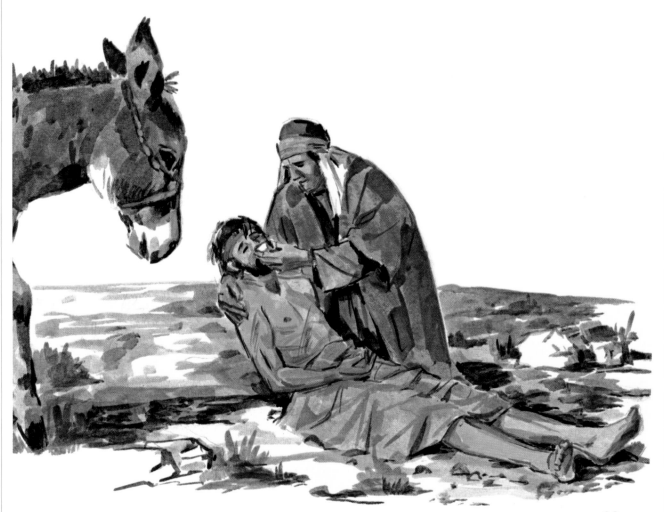

came by. He took one look at the poor man and went on his way.

"At last a Samaritan came down the road. As you know, you people all hate the Samaritans. You think they are not as good as you are. But when he saw this poor man lying beside the road, he felt sorry for him. He knelt down, put some medicine on his wounds, and bandaged them. Then he put the man on his donkey and took him to an inn. He took care of the man and paid for him to stay at the inn until he was well."

Then Jesus looked at the man who had tried to trick Him. "Now which of these men was a good neighbor?" He asked.

"The one who helped the man who needed him," he said.

"You must go and be like that Samaritan man," said Jesus. "That is the kind of neighbor you should be."

The Almost
Wasn't Helper

"Why do I have to go to the grocery store for Mommi?" Maxi grumbled all the way down the street. He was still grumbly when he came to the stoplight by the grocery store.

"Look at that lady by the stoplight," he complained. "She must be 80 years old and she went to the grocery store by herself. So why can't Mommi go?"

Maxi watched the lady for a while. The light turned green, and she started across the street. But when she heard a horn honk she quickly stepped back on the sidewalk. The light turned red, and the lady waited. But when it turned green she took one step into the street and then went back on the side-walk again.

"Looks like she needs some help crossing the street," Maxi said to himself. "Why doesn't someone help her? If I weren't in such a hurry, I would."

Maxi went into the grocery store. He bought the things on Mommi's list and started home. Then he saw the old lady, still waiting to cross the street.

"What's the matter with people?" Maxi grumbled. "Why doesn't someone help her?"

Maxi hurried down the street with his bag of groceries. But when he came to the end of the block, he looked back. The old lady was still standing there.

"I can't believe it!" he mumbled. "Still no one has helped her. Everyone has an excuse!"

Suddenly Maxi knew what he had said. Why couldn't HE help the lady? He wasn't REALLY in such a hurry, was he? He was making an excuse too.

Maxi hurried back to the lady. "May I help you cross the street?" he asked.

"What a sweet boy," the lady said with a smile. "I have cataracts and can't see well, so I really do need help to cross the street."

Maxi took the lady's arm. When the light turned green he led her across the street.

"Thank you! Thank you!" the lady said. "You are such a fine boy. Some other boy went into the grocery store and wouldn't stop to help me. Then another boy came out of the grocery store and he didn't stop to help me either. I'm so glad you are not like those thoughtless boys."

Maxi gulped. He was sorry he had been so thoughtless. Then he saw that the lady was holding a bag of groceries.

"Please let me carry your groceries home for you," he said.

The lady thanked Maxi all the way home. "You are a Good Samaritan," she said.

Maxi remembered the Bible story his family had read a few days before. The Good Samaritan helped a man who needed him.

"From now on I want to be a Good Samaritan helper," Maxi said. Then he waved good-bye and hurried home with Mommi's groceries.

Growing Is . . . Helping Someone Who Needs Us

What the Bible Story Teaches

A good helper helps a person who needs him most.

Thinking about the Bible Story

1. Why do you think the priest should have stopped to help the man?
2. Who did stop to help the man?
3. Why do you think the Samaritan is called The Good Samaritan?

What the Muffin Story Teaches

When you see someone who needs you, help that person.

Thinking about the Muffin Story

1. Why did Maxi not help the old woman at first? Why did he help her later?
2. If you were Maxi, what would you think when she said, "I'm so glad you are not like those thoughtless boys?"
3. What would you have thought when she said you were a Good Samaritan? What did she mean?

Who Should I Help Most?

1. The person who pays me most.
2. The person who needs me most.
3. The person who can help me most.

The Bible Says

How can you say you love God unless you help those who need you? (from 1 John 3:17).

Prayer

Dear Jesus, someone needs me today. Guide me to that person, then show me how I can help that person most. Amen.

Brothers Are Helpers

Exodus 4:18-31

"Please send someone to help me," Moses prayed. God had just asked Moses to lead His people away from Egypt. They were slaves there and God wanted them to leave.

"I can't do this by myself," Moses told God. "I can't talk well. I need a helper."

"I will help you talk," God promised. "I made your mouth, so I can help you use it."

"But I still need a helper," Moses begged.

"All right, I will send your brother Aaron to help you," God said. "He will go with you. He will talk for you. He will meet you here at Mount Sinai."

Moses was praying in the desert near Mount Sinai. He had seen a bush burning, but it never burned up. Moses knew that God was there. He had even heard God talk to him.

When God stopped talking, Moses hurried home. He told his father-in-law Jethro what had happened. He told Jethro that God was sending him to Egypt to lead his people away.

"Go," said Jethro. "You must do what God has commanded."

So Moses left Jethro and headed toward Egypt with his wife and son. But first he must stop at Mount Sinai. God had promised to send Aaron there to meet Moses.

When Moses came to Mount Sinai, there was Aaron, waiting for him. "God told me to meet you here to help you," Aaron said. "But how did you know I would be here?"

"Because God told me you would be here," Moses answered.

"You will help God set our people free," Aaron said. "And I will help you."

So the two brothers were two helpers. Moses would help God. Aaron would help Moses. And both would help each other.

Two Hundred Bricks and Four Helpers

"What are you doing, Charlie?"

"Moving 200 bricks, Maxi."

"How long will it take you?"

"TWO hours, Maxi."

"Want some help, Charlie? If I help you, we can move the bricks in ONE hour."

Just then, Pookie and BoBo came along. "What are you doing?" they asked.

"Moving 200 bricks," said Maxi. "I'm helping Charlie so it will take only ONE hour instead of TWO hours."

"Need some help?" asked BoBo. "If we both help, we can finish in ONE-HALF hour."

So Pookie moved 50 bricks.

BoBo moved 50 bricks.

Maxi moved 50 bricks.

And Charlie moved 50 bricks.

It did not take Charlie TWO hours. It did not take Charlie and Maxi ONE hour. It took

Charlie, Maxi, Pookie and BoBo ONE-HALF hour.

When they were all through, Charlie's mommi gave them a big pitcher of lemonade. "Why do you look so happy?" she asked.

"Because it's fun to be helpers," said Maxi. "Good helpers are happy helpers."

"You're right," said Charlie's mommi. "You each gave Charlie 50 bricks worth of help, but you each got 50 bricks worth of happiness."

"Then let's celebrate with 200 bricks worth of lemonade," said Maxi. That's a lot of happiness and lemonade, isn't it?

Growing Is . . .
Helping Each Other

What the Bible Story Teaches

When we help someone else, we often find that we help one another.

Thinking about the Bible Story

1. How did God want Moses to help him?
2. Why did Moses want someone else to help?
3. Who did God send to help Moses? How did these two men help each other?

What the Muffin Story Teaches

When we help each other we get our work done much faster. Then we have time to do fun things together.

Thinking about the Muffin Story

1. Why do you think Maxi helped Charlie? Why do you think Pookie and BoBo helped?
2. What happened when they all helped each other?
3. Who got 50 bricks worth of happiness? Why?

When Should We Help Each Other?

1. Only when someone asks us.
2. Only when someone pays us.
3. When someone needs us.

The Bible Says

Encourage one another and build one another up (from 1 Thessalonians 5:11).

Prayer

Dear Jesus, let me be Your helper. Then show me how to help You by helping others. Amen.